HISTORY AND GEOGRAPHY 103
I HAVE FEELINGS

CONTENTS

I. **I FEEL SAD** 2
   Times When I Feel Sad 2
   What to Do When I Feel Sad 16

II. **I FEEL AFRAID** 19
   Times When I Feel Afraid 20
   What to Do When I Feel Afraid 24

III. **I FEEL HAPPY** 28
   Times When I Feel Happy 28
   What to Do When I Feel Happy 32

IV. **I FEEL MANY THINGS** 35
   I Feel Angry 36
   I Feel Excited 38

Author: Mary Ellen Quint, Ph.D.
Editor: Rudolph Moore, Ph.D
Consulting Editor: Howard Stitt, Th.M., Ed.D.
Revision Editor: Alan Christopherson, M.S.

Alpha Omega Publications®

804 N. 2nd Ave. E., Rock Rapids, IA 51246-1759

© MCMXCVI by Alpha Omega Publications, Inc. All rights reserved. LIFEPAC, Doc Dickory, Dewey Decimole, Revver, Rikki, and Vicky Dickory are registered trademarks or trademarks of Alpha Omega Publications, Inc. pending registration in the United States Patent and Trademark Office. All rights reserved.

All trademarks and/or service marks referenced in this material are the property of their respective owners. Alpha Omega Publications, Inc. makes no claim of ownership to any trademarks and/or service marks other than their own and their affiliates', and makes no claim of affiliation to any companies whose trademarks may be listed in this material, other than their own.

Learn with our friends:

Hey! I am **Revver**. I like a lot of action.

Hello, boys and girls. I am **Doc**. Come and learn with my grandchildren.

I am **Vicky**, I love learning new things.

When you see me, I will help your teacher explain the exciting things you are expected to do.

When you do actions with me, you will learn how to write, draw, match words, read, and much more.

You and I will learn about matching words, listening, drawing, and other fun things in your lessons.

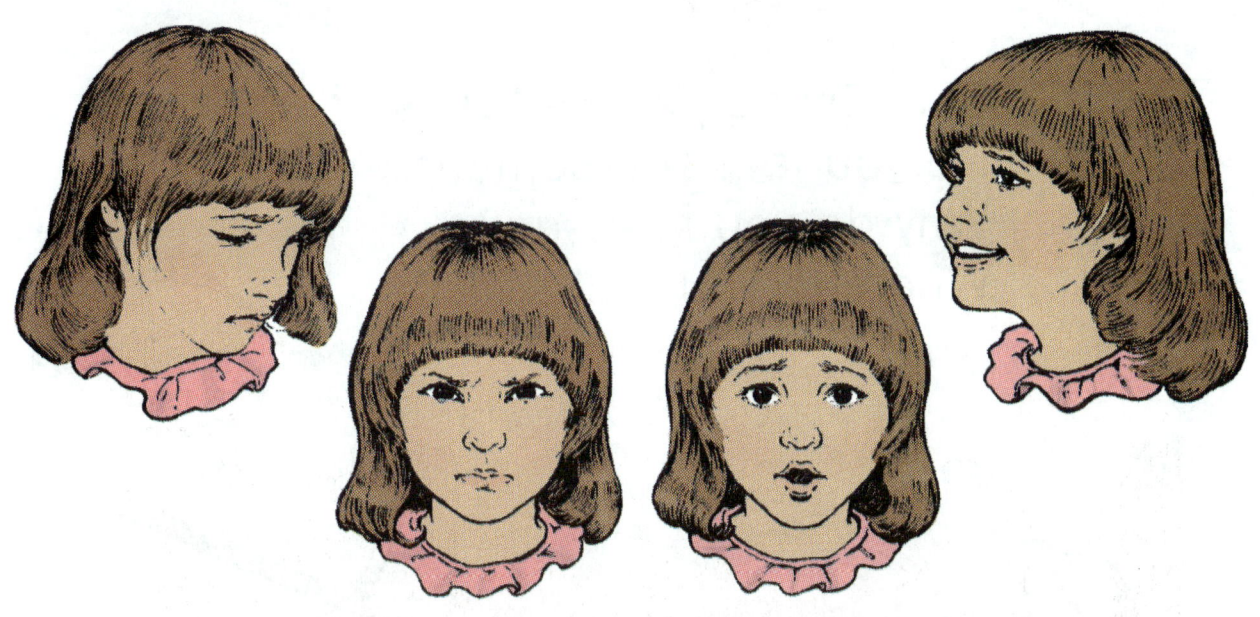

I HAVE FEELINGS

God gave you feelings.
You can feel many things.
You can feel sad or angry
or afraid or excited or happy
or many other things.

In this LIFEPAC®
you will read about feelings.

Objectives

1. I can tell what makes me feel sad.
2. I can tell what makes me feel afraid.
3. I can tell what makes me feel happy.
4. I can tell about other things I feel.

page 1 (one)

I. I FEEL SAD

Sometimes people feel sad.
Do you feel sad sometimes?
Why do you feel sad?
When do you feel sad?

TIMES WHEN I FEEL SAD

Sometimes I feel sad,
but I do not know why.
When do you feel sad?

I feel sad
    when I am all alone,
    when I have no one to
    play with me,
    when I am sick,
or when_____.

Tell what will happen next.

When do you feel sad?
How can you help someone else who is sad?

page 3 (three)

Jane Is Sick

Jane is my friend.
Jane is very sick.
She cannot go to school.
She cannot play.
She must stay in bed
all the time.

I feel sad
because Jane is sick.
I will make a picture for her.
I will pray for her.

Learn this Bible verse.

" ...I was sick, and ye visited me..."(Matthew 25:36)

Talk about the sick people that Jesus helped.

Draw a happy picture for a sick person. Color it. Copy it and give it to someone who is sick or sad.

Bob Is Little

Bob is my friend.
Bob is little.
Bob is smaller
than any of us.

Because Bob is little,
some children
make fun of him.
They call him names.
They make him cry.
They make me sad
because they hurt
my friend Bob.

God wants me to help Bob.
I want to do what
God wants.

How can you help Bob?
What can you say to him?
What can you do for him?

Circle yes or no.

Bob is little.   yes / no

I call Bob names.   yes / no

Some children made
Bob cry.   yes / no

God wants me to
help Bob.   yes / no

Some Days It Is Hard To Be Good

John felt sad
as he got ready for bed.
He did not know why.

As he said his prayers,
he still felt sad.
He began to think about his day.
Everything had gone wrong.

First, he disobeyed Mother's
orders to go straight to school.
He stopped at the park
and lost his new jacket there.

Next, John had a fight with Joe.
Joe had a new book
from the library.
John wanted the book, too.
He did not want
to wait for Joe to finish.

So John started a fight.
The book was torn.
The teacher became angry.
John had to stay
after school.

Circle the right word.

John felt_____.
happy / sad

John_____his mother.
obeyed / disobeyed

John_____his jacket.
lost / found

John had a fight with_____.
Jim / Joe

The book was_____.
open / torn

John had to stay_____school.
after / out of

Write 1, 2, 3 to show what happens first, next, and last.

page 11 (eleven)

On the way home from school,
John had hurt his best friend, Dan.
Dan had a new bike.
It was just like the one
John really wanted.

John knew he should be happy
for Dan, but he was not happy.
He felt sad and angry and grumpy.
He pushed Dan's new bike.
CRASH! It fell to the ground.
The shiny new bike
had a big scratch on it.

Dan cried.
John knew he had
hurt Dan, but he just laughed
and walked away.

"Why did I do that?"
thought John.
"Dan is my best friend.
He wanted a new bike
for a long time.
Why did I hurt him?"

Now John knew
why he felt sad.
He had done
so many things wrong.

"I am sorry, Jesus.
I did not want to be mean.
Please forgive me.
Please help me to be kind."

John got into bed.
He did not feel sad now.
He felt happy.
He turned out the light
and went to sleep.

Draw what you think John did when he saw Dan the next day.

Do you ever feel like John? What do you do about it?

15 (fifteen)

WHAT TO DO WHEN I FEEL SAD

When I feel sad,
I can
- draw a funny picture,
- visit a friend,
- read a good book,
- help someone,
- surprise someone,

or _____
_____

When I feel sad,
I can ask God to help me
feel glad.

Draw something that you do when you feel sad.

Talk about your picture.
Write about it in your tablet.

SELF TEST 1

Write 1, 2, 3 to show what happens <u>first</u>, <u>next</u>, and <u>last</u>.

Circle the right word.

Joe and John had a _____.
bike   /   fight

I can _____ someone who is sad.
help / hurt

"I was sick and ye _____ me."
left   /   visited

Tell your teacher one thing you do if you are sad.

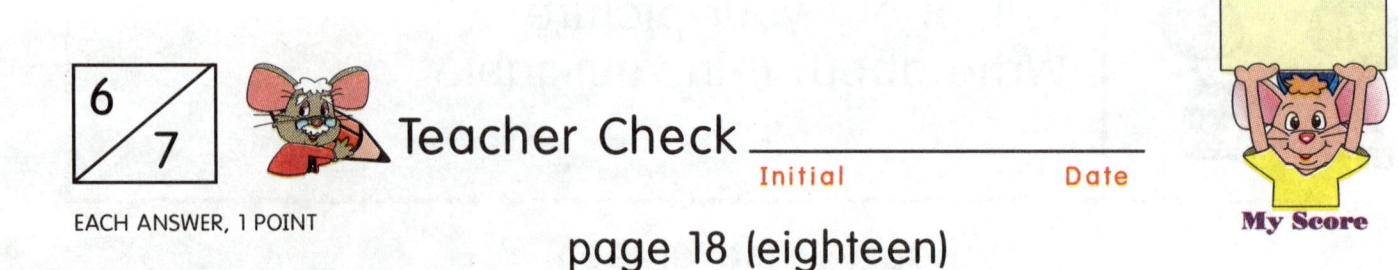

Teacher Check _____
            Initial   Date

6/7

EACH ANSWER, 1 POINT

page 18 (eighteen)

II. I FEEL AFRAID

Sometimes, I feel afraid.
Do you feel afraid sometimes?
When do you feel afraid?

TIMES WHEN I FEEL AFRAID

When are you afraid?
I feel afraid
    sometimes when I am alone,
    when it is dark,
    when someone hurts me,
    when my mother is sick,
    when I have a bad dream,
or when_____.

HISTORY & GEOGRAPHY 103

LIFEPAC TEST

10/12

Name _____
Date _____
Score _____

HISTORY & GEOGRAPHY 103: LIFEPAC TEST

Match.

happy

sad

afraid

Write 1, 2, 3 to show what happens first, next, and last.

page 1 (one)

Circle the right word.

"I will fear no _____: for thou art with me."
                good / evil

"Happy is the man that _____ wisdom."
                findeth / lost

"I was sick, and ye _____ me."
                left / visited

I am sad when my friend is _____.
                sick / well

God will always _____ me.
                help / forget

Thank you, God, for _____.
                hurting / feelings

NOTES

Circle the answer.

Sometimes when I am alone, I feel_____.
happy / sad

When I am sick, I feel_____.
sad / happy

When I am lost, I feel_____.
afraid / sad

When I fight, I feel_____.
sad / afraid

When I hurt someone, I feel_____.
sad / afraid

The First Day

Katy was new in school.
Today was her first day.
Katy was afraid.
She felt all alone.
She did not know anyone.
She felt afraid
 of the new children,
 of the new building, and
 of the new teacher.
Why did Katy feel afraid?
Would you feel afraid?

Help Katy find her way to school, to the chapel, and to the playground.

WHAT TO DO WHEN I FEEL AFRAID

When I feel afraid
of the dark,
I close my eyes
and think of sunshine.
What do you do?
When a bad dream
makes me feel afraid,
I tell Mom and Dad
about it.
What do you do?

When I hear stories
about the devil,
I feel afraid.
I ask God
to help me to do
what He wants me to do.
I am not afraid of God.
What do you do?

Learn this Bible verse.

"...I will fear no evil:
for thou art with me...."
(Psalm 23:4)

Write the verse in your tablet.

Talk about the memory verse.

Circle yes or no.

God will always help me.   yes / no

I am afraid of God.   yes / no

I ask God to help me.   yes / no

SELF TEST 2

Circle the answer.

Sometimes I am sad when I am _____.

alone / sleeping

I feel afraid when I have a _____.

bad dream / good day

God will _____ help me.

never / always

Say the verse you learned. (Psalm 23:4).

Circle the picture of someone who is sad.

Tell your teacher one thing you do if you are afraid.

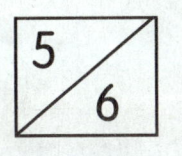

Teacher Check _____
Initial   Date

EACH ANSWER, 1 POINT

5/6

III. I FEEL HAPPY

I feel happy many times.
Do you feel happy?
When do you feel happy?

TIMES WHEN I FEEL HAPPY

When are you happy?
I feel happy
    when I do something good,
    when I do my work well, and
    when Mom or Dad give me a hug.

I feel happy
> when I say my prayers,
> when I learn something new,
> when I see a pretty flower, and
> when_____
> _____.

Draw something that makes you feel happy.

Talk about your picture.

page 30 (thirty)

Write 1, 2, 3 to show what happens first, next, and last.

page 31 (thirty-one)

WHAT TO DO WHEN I FEEL HAPPY

When I feel happy,
    I thank God.
    I try to make
    someone else happy, too.
    I draw a happy picture.
What do you do?

Learn this Bible verse.

"Happy is the man that findeth wisdom..." (Proverbs 3:13)

Write this verse in your tablet.

Talk about this verse.

Draw a picture of what you do when you are happy.

page 33 (thirty-three)

SELF TEST 3

Write 1, 2, 3 to show what happens first, next, and last.

Circle the right word.

"I was _____, and ye visited me."
  sad / sick

"I will fear _____ evil: for thou art with me."
  no / all

"_____ is the man that findeth wisdom."
  Sad / Happy

Tell your teacher one thing you do when you are happy.

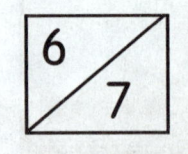

6/7

Teacher Check _____
          Initial   Date

EACH ANSWER, 1 POINT

page 34 (thirty-four)

IV. I FEEL MANY THINGS

I feel many things.
Sometimes I do not
feel happy or sad
or afraid.
Sometimes I feel angry.
Sometimes I feel excited.
Sometimes I feel _____
_____.

I FEEL ANGRY

One day
I made a big house of blocks.
My little brother knocked it down.
He did not mean to do it,
but I felt angry.

Jesus talked about brothers who were angry. He said that you must make up with your brother before you can come to Him (Matthew 5:21 through 24).

Paul says that if you are angry you should not stay that way. You should stop being angry before the day ends (Ephesians 4:26).

Listen to your teacher read these two parts from the Bible.

Talk about what Jesus and Paul said.

Write a prayer in your Tablet asking God to help you when you are angry. Your teacher will help you.

I FEEL EXCITED

Today is a special day.
Mother promised me
a surprise.
I feel excited.
I wonder what it is.
What do you think it is?

Draw a picture of something that makes you feel excited.

page 39 (thirty-nine)

SELF TEST 4

Write 1, 2, 3 to show what happens first, next, and last.

Match the picture and word.

afraid

happy

sad

page 40 (forty)

Circle the right word.

I am happy when I do something _____.
　　　　　　　　　　　　　　　　　　good / bad

I am sad when I _____ someone.
　　　　　　　help / hurt

Paul said to stop being angry before the
_____ends.
　day / week

Say two of the Bible verses that you learned to your teacher.

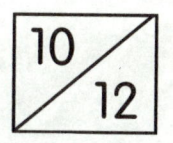

Teacher Check _____
　　　　　　　Initial　　　Date

NOTES